China's Ethnic Minorities

Foreign Languages Press   Beijing

"Culture of China" Editorial Board:
Consultants: Cai Mingzhao, Zhao Changqian, Huang Youyi, Liu Zhibin
Chief Editor: Xiao Xiaoming
Members of the Editorial Board: Xiao Xiaoming, Li Zhenguo, Tian Hui, Hu Baomin, Fang Yongming, Hu Kaimin, Cui Lili, Lan Peijin

Written by: Xing Li, Liao Pin, Yu Bingqing, Lan Peijin
Photographers: Du Dianwen, Xie Jun, Liu Sigong, Li Chunsheng, Cheng Weidong, Li Zhisen, Lan Peijin, Dan Zeng, Liu Jianming, Shen Jun, Gao Mingyi, Jiang Jian, Yuan Xuejun, Sun Yongxue, et al.
Translated by: Wang Qin, Ouyang Weiping
English Text Editor: Yu Ling
Designers: Yuan Qing, et al.
Editor: Lan Peijin

First Edition 2003

China's Ethnic Minorities

ISBN 7-119-03184-8

© Foreign Languages Press
Published by Foreign Languages Press
24 Baiwanzhuang Road, Beijing 100037, China
Home Page: http://www.flp.com.cn
E-mail Addresses: info@flp.com.cn
　　　　　　　　　sales@flp.com.cn
Distributed by China International Book Trading Corporation
35 Chegongzhuang Xilu, Beijing 100044, China
P.O. Box 399, Beijing, China

Printed in the People's Republic of China

China's Ethnic Minorities

China's Ethnic Minorities

China was a unitary multi-ethnic state as early as in the Qin Dynasty (221-207 BC). But at that time, Qin rule embraced only the agricultural areas along the Yangtze River, the Yellow River and the middle and lower reaches of the Pearl River, while in the vast area of northern China lived a vigorous nomadic people — the Hun ethnic group. The territory of the Hun tribes ranged from the Greater and Lesser Xing'an Mountains in the east to the Qilian Mountains, and even as far as the Tianshan Mountains in the west. The Great Wall, the construction of which had started as far back as the Warring States Period (475-221BC), divided China basically into agricultural and pastoral areas. However, the Great Wall could not separate the two areas completely. Their thriving animal husbandry, including the breeding of horses, brought the Hun people into close commercial contact with the Han Dynasty (206 BC-AD 220). Together with other nationalities they had a frequent presence in the Central Plains (comprising the middle and lower reaches of the Yellow River), promoting communication and integration between the southern agricultural area and northern pastoral area. This indicates that all the nationalities in China at that time developed the territory of the Chinese nation and at the same time together constructed Chinese culture. When the Huaxia, Youmiao and Baiyue peoples were building their civilizations in the Yellow and Yangtze River valleys, the ancestors of many other ethnic groups were creating their own civilizations in China's border areas.

With a history of more than 5,000 years, today China has 56 ethnic groups. In addition to the Han people, who form the majority of the population, there are 55 minority nationalities. Because they maintain an equal, harmonious and fraternal relationship with the Han people, they are called "fraternal nationalities." They are also called "minority" nationalities because their populations are relatively small in comparison to the Han population.

Although the 55 minority nationalities make up only 6.7% of China's population, they live in areas constituting 50%-60% of the total land area of the country. For historical reasons, most of the minority people live in the frontier provinces and regions. In the course of history, the different nationalities have made uneven progress in social, economic and cultural aspects. Thus, even in the mid-20th century, some minority nationalities still lived in conditions similar to those of the late stage of primitive society or slave society, while others were in the transitional phase from slave to feudal society or were at the stage of feudal society. After the founding of the People's Republic of China in 1949, the Central Government adopted steps to reform and develop production in the minority-nationality areas, enabling the local people to leap over several stages of social development and enter socialist society.

The 55 ethnic minorities use more than 80 languages, classified as members of the Han-Tibetan, Altaic, Austronesian, Indo-European and other language families. Many of the ethnic minorities developed indigenous scripts with which to write their own languages, but only 30 of the traditional ones are still in existence. Tibetan writing dates from the seventh century; the Bai and Zhuang scripts first appeared during the Tang (681-907) and Song dynasties (960-1279), respectively; the Mongol, Dai, Uygur, Kazak, and Kirgiz scripts were formed in the 13th century; the Yi and Yao forms of writing date from a very early period in the history; and in the 17th century,

Manchu and Xibo scripts appeared. The Dongba characters of the Naxi nationality and Shui characters of the Shui nationality are particularly interesting as they are pictographic ones, and are still in use today. Following Liberation in 1949, scientific scripts were invented for over 20 minority nationalities whose languages had previously had no written form, such as those of the Miao, Dong, Va, Li, Tujia, Buyi and Hani.

From ancient times, these ethnic minorities have been living scattered across the vast territory of China in compact communities. Located in different geographical environments, they promoted economic development in the light of local circumstances, creating Chinese civilization as a whole. Experts have affirmed that the Gaomiao site inhabited by the Dong people at Qianyang on the middle reaches of the Yuanjiang River is a relic of the paddy rice cultivation culture of more than 7,000 years ago. A great number of pottery pieces bearing patterns of the sun, birds, flowers and trees, etc. have been unearthed there. According to legend, it was birds that brought the Dong people corn seeds. The 9,000-year-old Pengtoushan Mountain Culture of the Tujia people of Hunan Province is also thought to belong to the paddy rice culture phase. Pottery shards discovered there display patterns of the sun, the moon and flowers, which are characteristic of the paddy rice culture. In the low mountains and river valleys in the west and southwest of Yunnan Province, the Jingpo, Achang, Yi, Blang and Jino ethnic groups developed paddy rice cultivation on terraced fields in the distant past. Textual research shows that perhaps it was the ancestors of the Dai nationality that first grew paddy rice in China. The Hani nationality is famed for cultivating tea bushes, some of which produce Pu'er tea, which is called "green gold." There are plenty of tea bushes over 100 years old still flourishing there. The She nationality also has a centuries-long history of cultivating tea bushes. The Huiming tea of Zhejiang Province, Oolong tea of Guangdong Province and Beiling tea of Fujian Province, all produced by members of the She nationality, enjoy great popularity. Huiming tea was an item of tribute during the Ming and Qing dynasties and was awarded a gold medal at the 1915 Panama International Exhibition. Chinese ethnic groups have made numerous other inventions and contributions in the economic field.

Chinese civilization has both an agricultural and a stockbreeding tradition: The former was the common fruit of the Han and other nationalities, while the latter was engaged in mainly by minority nationalities. There are vast grasslands in northeast China, ranging from the Xing'an Mountains westwards to Central Asia, via the Yinshan and Tianshan mountain ranges in the Xinjiang Uygur Autonomous Region. From the Tianshan Mountains to the Qinghai-Tibet Plateau a crescent-shaped pastoral area extends to the Zhongdian area in Yunnan. This crescent is today home to some modern nomadic peoples, such as the Mongol, Ewenki, Kazak, Kirgiz and Tibet. In the Yinshan and Tianshan Mountains, ancient rock paintings record the history of the domestication of the horse, cow, yak, goat, sheep, donkey, mule and camel by ethnic-minority nomads. The latter paid particular attention to horse breeding, and for centuries would barter fine horses for tea produced in the agricultural areas of south China.

In the field of textiles, indispensable for clothing and furnishings, since ancient times the Han people of the Central Plains have enjoyed a universal reputation for their accomplishments in silkworm breeding, silk reeling and silk weaving, while cotton textiles were developed by ethnic minorities. The Li people of Hainan Province are especially skilled at weaving. In the 13th century, the famous Han weaver Huang Daopo traveled to remote Yazhou [today's Sanya City on Hainan Island] and learned the technique of making fine cotton cloth from Li women. She then spread it to Jiangsu and Zhejiang provinces, promoting the development of the cotton textile industry in the Central Plains. Beautiful brocades made by the Zhuang, Li, Dong and Dai minorities were first produced more than 1,000 years ago.

The Li, Miao and Yao peoples in the south also made many kinds of textiles such as Boluo cloth, Mao (hawksbill) cloth, Zhu cloth [light blue or white fine cotton cloth], Yaoban cloth [blue batik with white speckles], ramie cloth and kapok cloth. The bright and colorful patterns of these types of cloth demonstrate the diverse characteristics of the different nationalities. Wax printing is a unique technique invented by certain of China's ethnic minorities for printing and dyeing hand-made cloth. The patterns emerge natural and pretty, with a clear distinction between blue and white. As wax shows natural cracks after cooling off, after dyeing wax printing produces an unusual decorative effect with distinctive ethnic features. In addition, China's embroidery enjoys a high reputation throughout the world, especially that of the country's Miao, Li, Dong and Bai nationalities.

The minority people's great accomplishments in the crafts of weaving and embroidery are fully demonstrated in their local costumes. Their clothes are of high-quality materials, excellent workmanship and dazzling splendor. Since these ethnic groups live in different regions and engage in various kinds of productive labor, their clothes are of diverse designs. For instance, the northern nationalities inhabiting the Mongolian Plateau, Qinghai-Tibet Plateau and Xinjiang Basin pasture land usually wear long garments, which are quite different in design for each nationality. The Mongols wear a loose garment with long sleeves, colorful edging and the lower hem covering the feet. The Tibetan robe is looser than that of the Mongols, with the left lapel bigger than the right one. The Uygur usually wear a kind of Chinese-style cotton coat, with a stiff collar, no buttons, and the lower hem extending to the knee. This kind of garment is called *qiapan*. The Kazak people wear a light and warm overcoat made of camel's hair, called *kupu*. The Hezhen group, living along the downstream of the Heilongjiang River, lived by fishing in the past, so their traditional garments are made of fish skin. The Manchu men's traditional clothes is a long gown and mandarin jacket, while the women's is a loose cheongsam reaching to the ankle. In the early 20th century, the cheongsam evolved into a close-fitting dress extending below the knee with high neck, narrow sleeves, slender waist and two slits on the left and right, buttoning down the right side. The unique design is graceful and elegant, displaying the beautiful figures of eastern women.

Both men and women of the minority nationalities living in southern China and engaging in farming usually wear skirts. They vary greatly in design and pattern. Generally speaking, the Yi, Dong, Miao, Lisu, Bouyei, Primi and De'ang nationalities wear long skirts, while the Dai, Zhuang, Gaoshan, Blang, Lahu, Gelao and Li nationalities, straight ones, and the Hani, Li, Jino and Va nationalities, short ones. The long and short skirts also show differences in the placing of pleats in different regions. The upper three parts of the long skirt of the Yi nationality are made of cloth of different colors. The fourth part is pleated. The long Dai and Primi skirts drag along the ground, with the former folded in the upper part and close-fitting in the waist, while the latter is spread out and flowing in the lower part. The Gelao straight skirt of modern times is made of a whole piece of blue cloth, retaining its ancient simplicity. The Li women of tropical Hainan Island wear skirts which extend only to the knee, making them convenient for work in paddy fields. Of those wearing short skirts, the Hani women wear pleated black short skirts, the pleated skirts of the Miao in southeastern Guizhou are only 30 cm long, and the Shui women wear short trousers underneath their skirts.

The architecture of ethnic minorities shows distinct national and local features. The nomads among the Mongolians and Tibetans, roaming the frigid 3,000-m-high Qinghai-Tibet Plateau, live in white or black felt tents. The Tibetan and Qiang nationalities are expert at constructing watchtower-like buildings. The buildings of the Zhuang, Bouyei, Dong and Shui communities in southern Yunnan, southern

Guizhou and southern Hunan are all of wooden structure and have railings. The Li live in boat-shaped houses with railings, ingeniously constructed and unique in design. The villages of the Dong nationality are noted for their drum towers and covered bridges.

As far as art is concerned, China's minority nationalities have a tradition as long and splendid as that of the Han. Rock paintings executed by ancient tribespeople, discovered in the Yinshan Mountains of Inner Mongolia, the Huashan Mountains in Guangxi and Hutubi County in Xinjiang, are masterpieces of primitive expression. Throughout China's history, there was no lack of minority painters enjoying equal fame with their Han counterparts. Murals in temples of the Lamaist faith built in large numbers since the 15th century, mostly found in Tibetan- and Mongolian-nationality areas of western China, are unique and outstanding works of painting. Those in the Potala Palace in Lhasa, in particular, are famed for their grand composition, bright colors and diverse forms of expression. Tangkha (scroll pictures) are another genre related to Lamaism. The picture is outlined on cloth or silk, and then filled in with colors made of special plant and mineral materials produced in Tibet. Tangkha can be classified into four categories: embroidered Tangkha, jacquard Tangkha, applique Tangkha and precious-bead Tangkha. The latter are decorated with pearls, coral, turquoise, gold and silver, and are rare treasures.

Chinese minority people are expert singers and dancers. Many of their songs, dances and musical pieces enjoy high reputations both at home and abroad. Northern songs are resounding and powerful; in particular, the Mongolian pastoral songs are slow, melodious and deep. Southern music and songs are cheerful and unrestrained, for instance, epitomized by the Dong people's Dage and the Zhuang people's Paige songs. The *Twelve Mukam* and *Thirteen Melodies for Stringed Instruments* of the Uygur are rare and precious relics of Chinese folk music. Among dances, the most famous are the Peacock Dance of the Dai, the Hair-tossing Dance of the Gaoshan, the Hand-in-Hand Group Circle Dance of the Dong, the Wooden Drum Dance of the Va, the Reed-pipe Dance of the Miao, and the Horse Dance, Eagle Dance and Milking Dance of the Mongolians. The literature of ethnic minorities is rich in form and vitality. The thrilling love songs, earth-shaking epics and countless folk tales passed down from generation to generation contain the essence of the culture, spirit and wisdom of China's ethnic minorities. The three great epics – *The Epic of King Gesar*, *Manas* and *Janger*, have enjoyed continuous popularity for centuries, and can take their rightful place among other epic masterpieces of international literature.

In the fields of science and technology, minority ethnic groups have produced many outstanding and talented people. Emperor Xianzong (reigned 1251-1260) of the Yuan Dynasty, of the Mongolian nationality, was the first person in China to study Euclid's treatise on geometry. Another Mongolian, Ming Antu, in the 18th century was the first person in China to devise a method of calculating Pi (π) and wrote a four-volume book on it. Emperor Kangxi of the Qing Dynasty (reigned 1662-1722), of the Manchu nationality, was also an accomplished mathematician. In addition, he was the chief compiler of *The Origins of the Calendric System, Music and Mathematics*, in 100 volumes. Ethnic groups were not behind the Han in astronomical observations and produced accurate calendars centuries ago. The Dai Calendar, the Tibetan Calendar, the Ordos Calendar of the Mongols and the Yi Calendar are all crystallizations of the wisdom of these nationalities. The famous Hui astronomer Jamal al-Din in the 13th century made an armillary sphere, azimuth compass and celestial globe, and supervised the compilation of *The Illustrated Geological Annals*. Another outstanding Mongolian scholar, Li Siguang (1889-1971), was the founder of geomechanics, exploring a new approach for probing the structure and movements of the earth's crust.

In the field of medicine, too, minority-nationality people have accumulated rich knowledge. The Tibetan, Mongolian, Uygur, Kazak and Korean nationalities have all produced systematic bodies of medical knowledge, and the Zhuang, Yi, Dai and Li have made important contributions to medical science. Yuthok Yonten Gonpo compiled the achievements of Tibetan medicine in the *Four Medical Classics*. On the basis of this work, 79 colored wall charts were made to assist in the diagnosis of ailments and the identification of drugs.

There is a long history of friendly contacts and cultural exchanges between the nomadic lifestyle of the minority nationalities and the farming lifestyle of the Central Plains. Advanced techniques practiced in the Central Plains, such as silkworm breeding and silk reeling, and artificial irrigation, were spread into the areas inhabited by the nomadic ethnic minorities. An example of the latter technique is Xinjiang's "karez," which is an irrigation and drinking water well system involving a series of underground channels. In the seventh century, when the Tang Dynasty (618-907) Princess Wencheng went to Tibet to marry King Songtsen Gampo, she took with her many advanced techniques from the Central Plains, such as vegetable planting, pottery making, wine making and metallurgy. At the same time, some breeds of livestock developed in pastoral areas were carried into agricultural areas, which consequently improved the local farming techniques. Horses, musk, livestock, lacquerware and fine swords were brought into the Central Plains from the ethnic-minority areas of southwestern China, in exchange for porcelain, medicinal herbs, brocade and silks, and handicrafts. From ancient times to the present, ethnic minorities and the Han people have always supplied each other's needs, and integrated and develop mutually in the course of interchanges and communication.

The homelands of the minority peoples are mostly border areas of China, and therefore these regions serve as a link between China and other countries. The Xinjiang Uygur Autonomous Region, inhabited by more than 20 nationalities at present, was called the Western Regions in ancient times, and was a bridge facilitating communication between the eastern and western civilizations. The "Silk Road" from Xi'an in Shaanxi Province at the eastern end to Central Asia, the Black Sea, the Mediterranean Sea and as far as Rome at the farthest western end, ran through the Gansu Corridor along two roads lying to the south and north, respectively, of the Tarim Basin, south of the Tianshan Mountains, and then cut across Congling Ridge. In fact, there was a much older "Silk Road" running from Sichuan Province to Myanmar and India via Yunnan Province, largely inhabited by ethnic minorities. In ancient times, this ancient road was not only one linking southern China with other parts of the world, but also a corridor for ethnic groups to travel south or north. These two channels allowed the scientific knowledge, music, art, western Christianity, Islam from Western Asia and Buddhism from India to gradually spread into the Central Plains. At the same time, China's traditional culture and science and technology, and even some handicrafts such as silk, porcelain, tea and jade ware, were carried to countries in Southeast Asia and the West.

Population and Areas of Distribution of the Ethnic Minorities in China

(Based on the Fourth National Census, July 1, 1990)

Name	Population	Areas of Distribution	Name	Population	Areas of Distribution
Mongolian	4,802,400	Inner Mongolia, Xinjiang, Liaoning, Jilin, Heilongjiang, Gansu, Hebei, Henan, Qinghai	Shui	347,100	Guizhou, Guangxi
			Dongxiang	373,700	Gansu, Xinjiang
			Naxi	277,800	Yunnan, Sichuan
Hui	8,612,000	Ningxia, Gansu, Henan, Hebei, Qinghai, Shandong, Yunnan, Xinjiang, Anhui, Liaoning, Heilongjiang, Jilin, Shaanxi, Beijing, Tianjin	Jingpo	119,300	Yunnan
			Kirgiz	143,500	Xinjiang, Heilongjiang
			Tu	192,600	Qinghai, Gansu
			Daur	121,500	Inner Mongolia, Heilongjiang, Xinjiang
Tibetan	4,593,100	Tibet, Qinghai, Sichuan, Gansu, Yunnan	Mulam	160,600	Guangxi
			Qiang	198,300	Sichuan
Uygur	7,207,000	Xinjiang	Blang	82,400	Yunnan
Miao	7,383,600	Guizhou, Hunan, Yunnan, Guangxi, Sichuan, Hainan, Hubei	Salar	87,500	Qinghai, Gansu
			Maonan	72,400	Guangxi
Yi	6,578,500	Sichuan, Yunnan, Guizhou, Guangxi	Gelao	438,200	Guizhou, Guangxi
			Xibe	172,900	Xinjiang, Liaoning, Jilin
Zhuang	15,555,800	Guangxi, Yunnan, Guangdong, Guizhou	Achang	27,700	Yunnan
			Primi	29,700	Yunnan
Bouyei	2,548,300	Guizhou	Tajik	33,200	Xinjiang
Korean	1,923,400	Jilin, Liaoning, Heilongjiang	Nu	27,200	Yunnan
Manchu	9,846,800	Liaoning, Jilin, Heilongjiang, Hebei, Beijing, Inner Mongolia	Uzbek	14,800	Xinjiang
			Russians	13,500	Xinjiang
Dong	2,508,600	Guizhou, Hunan, Guangxi	Ewenki	26,400	Inner Mongolia, Heilongjiang
Yao	2,137,000	Guangxi, Hunan, Yunnan, Guangdong, Guizhou	De'ang	15,500	Yunnan
			Bonan	11,700	Gansu
Bai	1,598,100	Yunnan, Guizhou	Yugur	12,300	Gansu
Tujia	5,725,000	Hunan, Hubei	Jing	18,700	Guangxi
Hani	1,254,800	Yunnan	Tatar	5,100	Xinjiang
Kazak	1,110,800	Xinjiang, Gansu, Qinghai	Drung	5,800	Yunnan
Dai	1,025,400	Yunnan	Oroqen	7,000	Inner Mongolia, Heilongjiang
Li	1,112,500	Hainan	Hezhen	4,300	Heilongjiang
Lisu	574,600	Yunnan, Sichuan	Moinba	7,500	Tibet
Va	352,000	Yunnan	Lhoba	2,300	Tibet
She	634,700	Fujian, Zhejiang, Jiangxi, Guangdong	Jino	18,000	Yunnan
Gaoshan	2,900	*Taiwan, Fujian	* The population figure for the Gaoshan does not include the Gaoshan in Taiwan Province.		
Lahu	411,500	Yunnan			

Contents

1. The Mongolians 12
2. The Hui 16
3. The Tibetans 18
4. The Uygur 22
5. The Miao 25
6. The Yi 30
7. The Zhuang 32
8. The Koreans 33
9. The Bouyei 34
10. The Manchu 36
11. The Dong 38
12. The Yao 41
13. The Bai 44
14. The Tujia 46
15. The Hani 48
16. The Kazak 50
17. The Li 53
18. The Dai 54
19. The Lisu 57
20. The Va 58
21. The She 60
22. The Gaoshan 61
23. The Lahu 62
24. The Shui 64
25. The Dongxiang 67
26. The Naxi 68
27. The Jingpo 71
28. The Kirgiz 73
29. The Daur 75
30. The Tu 76
31. The Mulam 79
32. The Qiang 80
33. The Blang 82
34. The Salar 84
35. The Maonan 85
36. The Xibe 86
37. The Gelao 88
38. The Primi 89
39. The Achang 90
40. The Tajik 92
41. The Nu 94
42. The Uzbek 96
43. The Ewenki 97
44. The Russians 100
45. The Bonan 101
46. The De'ang 102
47. The Yugur 104
48. The Jing 107
49. The Tatar 108
50. The Drung 109
51. The Oroqen 110
52. The Hezhen 112
53. The Moinba 114
54. The Lhoba 115
55. The Jino 116

蒙古族 The Mongolians

Half of the Mongolian population of China lives in the Inner Mongolia Autonomous Region in the border area of northern China. The others are mostly found in every province and region in the northwest of China. The autonomous region is adorned with large stretches of beautiful grassland and several ranges of mountains on the border between the eastern and central parts. Traditionally, the Mongolians led a nomadic life, taking their herds of cattle and sheep to pasture according to the patterns of the seasons. Some still follow this traditional lifestyle. The Mongolian aristocrat Timujin (1167-1227) united all the Mongolian tribes and founded the Mongol Khanate. After several military campaigns launched westwards and southwards, the Mongolians founded the Yuan Dynasty (1271-1368), reuniting China and putting an end to a chaotic situation that had lasted for more than 200 years. They made Dadu (today's Beijing) the capital of the dynasty.

Look! A bride!

A Mongolian bride.

The *aobao* (heap of sand, stone or earth laid out as a road marker or boundary sign by Mongolians, formerly also worshipped as a habitation of spirits) on Aobao Mountain in Dong Ujimqin Banner is the most famous one on the Mongolian grassland. A sacrifice is held here on the third day of the sixth month by the lunar calendar every year.

Buryat Mongolian women at the Nadam Fair.

Wrestling is a favorite Mongolian sport.

13

A Mongolian family on the Xilin Gol Grassland.

Hospitable Mongolians.

A milkmaid.

回族 The Hui

The Hui are the second-biggest ethnic minority in China, after the Zhuang. People of the Hui nationality can be found in almost every part of China, but the largest concentration of them is in the Ningxia Hui Autonomous Region, in northwest China.

The Hui are followers of Islam, and this tradition has had a great impact on their economy, culture, social life, and habits and customs. They normally use the Han language, but between themselves or on some special religious occasions they use some Arabic or Persian terms.

The prayer hall of the Ox Street Mosque in Beijing can hold over 1,000 people.

A Hui girl.

Old Hui men love wearing big glasses.

A Hui singer at a *hua'er* folksong performance.

A literacy class for women held in the Old King Mosque in Linxia, Gansu Province.

藏族 The Tibetans

The emergence of the Tibetans on the Qinghai-Tibet Plateau can be traced back 5,000 years. This plateau in southwestern China is the highest in the world, with an average altitude of over 4,000 m. Apart from the Tibet Autonomous Region, Tibetan-nationality communities can be found in Qinghai, Sichuan, Gansu and Yunnan provinces.

The Tibetans believe in the Lamaist form of Buddhism, which has played a major role in formation of their unique culture, art and lifestyle.

Monks at a Buddhist service.

14. A sacred mountain and sutra streamers.

People holding small Buddhist prayer-wheels are a common sight in Tibet.

A Tibetan girl.

Tibetan people in Qinghai Province.

Tibetan people in Yunnan Province.

维吾尔族 The Uygur

The Uygur are the largest ethnic minority in the Xinjiang Uygur Autonomous Region. Making up three-fifths of Xinjiang's total population, they mostly live in the area south of the Tianshan Mountains.

The Uygur are descended from the nomads who roamed north and northwestern China in the third century. Historical records call them the Huihe. Natural calamities and wars at the end of the ninth century forced one group of Huihe move to the area around Turpan and Hami. Over the following centuries, they mingled with the natives of the area and the Tubo, Khitan and Mongolians who came later, and in 1934 they took the name Uygur.

The Uygur have their own spoken and written language, and they believe in Islam.

A Uygur carpet shop.   Uygur girls.

Uygur people celebrate their traditional Corban Festival ('Id al-Kurban) in Kashi.

Nang (a kind of crusty pancake) is a favorite traditional staple food of the Uygur.

Uygur people often wear colorful square caps.

Airing house for grapes in Turpan.

A harmonious Uygur family.

A traditional Uygur house.

苗族 The Miao

The Miao are a large minority distributed in Guizhou, Yunnan and western Hunan provinces. Small numbers of them live in western Hubei, Guangxi, Sichuan and Hainan provinces.

According to historical records, the ancestors of the Miao were already settled in western Hunan and eastern Guizhou during the Qin and Han dynasties, over 2,000 years ago. The Miao have their own spoken and written language, but most of them know the Han language. The customs and habits of the Miao are rather diversified in different areas, as they moved from place to place over the ages and lived in mixed communities with other nationalities.

Silver ornaments are favorite decorations of Miao girls.

Greeting toasts to approaching guests.

The clothes and personal ornaments of the Miao boast the finest workmanship and largest variety of all the costumes of China's nationalities. The Miao girls in the two pictures live in Duyun, Guizhou Province. Their silver headdresses and skirts are decorated with chicken feathers, and therefore they are called "chicken feather Miao."

A drum dance of the Miao people of western Hunan Province.

Most of the ethnic groups in southwestern China live in houses made of timber or bamboo and supported on stilts. The picture shows the Miao stockade in Shanglangde Village in the southeastern area of Guizhou Province.

A girl of the Gejia branch of the Miao.

Young Miao people prepare for the Miao New Year.

彝族 The Yi

The ancestors of the Yi people were already settled in Yunnan over 2,000 years ago. In the eighth century, the ancestors of the Yi and Bai nationalities founded the Kingdom of Nanzhao in the same area. Today, the Yi are the largest minority nationality in southwest China. Most of them live in Sichuan, Yunnan, Guizhou and Guangxi. The Liangshan Yi Autonomous Prefecture in Sichuan is the largest Yi community.

Most of the Yi engage in farming in the humid subtropical zone, but some raise domestic animals in woodland or grassland areas.

The Yi language exists in six dialects, written in an ancient syllabic script.

Young Yi people in the Xiaoliang Mountains in northwestern Yunnan.

Yi children in the Daliang Mountains of Sichuan.

Flower Festival of the Yi people of Yunnan.

The clothes worn by the Yi women in the Daliang Mountains of Sichuan are elegant and brightly colored.

The headdress worn by Yi women in Yuanmou, Yunnan, is made with about four kilograms of knitting wool.

壮族 *The Zhuang*

The Zhuang are the largest ethnic minority in China. Most of them live by farming in the Guangxi Zhuang Autonomous Region in southern China. They are thought to be descendents of "Liujiang Man," who lived over 50,000 years ago. The Zhuang have their own spoken and written language, but they mainly use the Han language.

Zhuang drama and brocade are outstanding features of the culture of this nationality, in addition to its rich folk literature and traditional songs and dances.

Zhuang girls

The Flower Lady of the Zhuang is a goddess in charge of child bearing.

A beautiful hometown of the Zhuang people—Lijiang in the Guangxi Zhuang Autonomous Region.

朝鲜族 The Koreans

The Korean minority in China are descendants of immigrants from the Korean Peninsula from the end of the 17th century. They have settled in Jilin, Liaoning and Heilongjiang provinces. The Yanbian Korean Autonomous Prefecture and Changbai Korean Autonomous County, in Jilin Province, are home to the largest community of Koreans.

The Koreans have their own spoken and written language, but many also know the Han language.

Seesawing is a traditional game for Korean women during holidays.

The Koreans have a fine tradition of respecting the old. The picture shows presents prepared for a man on his 60th birthday by his sons and grandsons.

布依族 The Bouyei

There are major Bouyei communities in central and southern Guizhou Province, and small numbers are found in the Wenshan area of Yunnan Province and the Ningnan area of Sichuan Province. The Bouyei homelands are characterized by many mountains and rivers, fertile soil and mild climate, and are famous for black glutinous rice and giant salamanders.

The spoken language of the Bouyei is similar to that of the Zhuang, Dai and Dong people, and has adopted some Han words. They have no written language.

A Bouyei wedding ceremony.

Typical Bouyei residences are made of stone. All Bouyei women are highly skilled at making batik.

Tea ceremony.

Heroes who drive away demons and evil spirits wear simple grass garments and hold fearsome weapons.

The "cleaning the stockade" activity of the Bouyei.

35

满族 The Manchu

The ancestors of the Manchu settled in the area of northeast China lying between the Heilongjiang and Ussuri rivers. They were originally called the Sushen or Mohe people, then in the tenth century they changed their name to Nüzhen, and founded the Jin Dynasty (1115-1234) which ruled the northern China. In the 17th century, following their leader Nurhachi, they expanded their territory both southwards and northwards. They began to call themselves Manchu in 1635, and founded the Qing Dynasty (1664-1911), the last of the feudal dynasties to rule China.

After the founding of the Qing Dynasty, large numbers of Manchu immigrated to the hinterland of China, adopting the customs and habits of the Han people. Only the Manchu living in their ancestral homeland still retain their traditional customs and language.

Elderly Manchu people do the Yangge dance, a popular rural folk dance in the northeast of China.

The Manchu put their babies to sleep in suspended cradles. This custom dates from the days when both Manchu men and women were hunters on horseback. They would suspend the cradles with the babies in from tree branches to keep them safe from wild animals while they were out hunting.

36

It is not uncommon among the Manchu for teenage girls to smoke pipes, and the elderly prefer long pipes.

A Manchu girl in her best clothes.

The Dong

The Dong live mainly in a contiguous area across the borders of Guizhou, Hunan and Guangxi provinces. They have their own spoken language, and use the Han language for writing.

The Dong are mainly farmers, with forestry as a sideline. Dong women are famous for their skill at weaving brocade and cloth that are both exquisite and durable. Dong villages are remarkable for their traditional drum towers and covered bridges.

A Dong girl in Liping, Guizhou Province.

The drum tower is an indispensable feature of the traditional Dong stockaded village. Each Dong clan builds its own drum tower. In the past, the drum tower was the place where clan affairs were discussed and decided.

The Dongs usually build their villages by water, and span rivers with covered bridges. The best-known one is the Chengyang Bridge in the Guangxi Zhuang Autonomous Region. The picture shows the Tongdao Bridge in southern Hunan Province.

A banquet held on a covered bridge.

A Dong costume dating from the Ming Dynasty(1368-1644).

Weaving.

40

瑶族 *The Yao*

The biggest concentration of Yao people is in Guangxi, but Hunan, Yunnan, Guangdong and Guizhou provinces also have large numbers of Yao.

Since the Qin and Han dynasties the ancestors of the Yao have lived in mountainous areas, engaging in agriculture and forestry. They have their own spoken and written language, but many use the Han, Zhuang or Dong languages. The Yao of different areas have distinct customs, lifestyles and costumes.

Stockaded villages are often found on steep hillsides.

The Pan Wang Dance of the Yao people of Yunnan Province.

A Yao girl in western Hunan Province.

The Red Yao of the Guangxi Zhuang Autonomous Region grow their hair long.

The traditional upper garment of Yao women in southern Guizhou consists of two connected pieces of cloth which hang in front of the chest and over the back. (Yao men wear white trousers, so they are called "White-trousered Yao.")

A Yao barn in southern Guizhou Province. The roof keeps off the rain, the floor is moisture-resistant and the overturned pottery jar in the middle keeps mice away.

The Yao people of Yaolu Village in the Dayao Mountains bury their dead in caves.

白族 The Bai

About 2,000 years ago, the ancestors of the Bai settled in the Dali area of Yunnan Province, living on fishing. In 937, Duan Siping founded the state of Dali. Most Bai people still live in the Dali area, while others are scattered in Guizhou, Sichuan and Hunan provinces.

The Bai have their own spoken and written language, but they also use the Han language. More than 90 percent of the Bai are engaged in agriculture, as their habitats include fertile farmland.

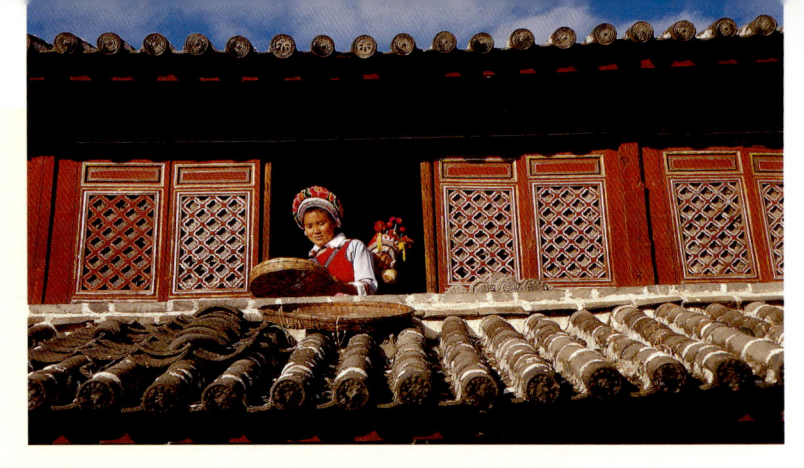

The central room of a traditional Bai house is made up of two stories. The ground floor is a sitting room, and the upper floor is for bedrooms.

Dressing a bride.

A wedding ceremony.

44

A typical Bai sitting room.

The fine art of Bai architecture is demonstrated in the construction of the gateway.

Placing the crossbeam of a new house.

45

土家族 **The Tujia**

The hilly areas of Hunan and western Hubei provinces are home to the descendants of the ancient Ba people, i.e. today's Tujia. Having mingled with the Han, Miao and Bai peoples for centuries, the Tujia mostly use the Han language, and only a small number, who live in remote villages, know the Tujia language.

Most of the Tujia worship a white tiger totem, although some Tujia in western Hunan worship a turtle totem.

The Tujia have a longstanding tradition of group dancing. The left picture shows a sacred "Maogusi" dance. The dancers are covered with straw to signify the reappearance of their ancestors, the so-called "hairy people." The upper picture shows a funeral overnight dance. The middle one is the hand-waving dance represented on a piece of embroidery.

46

The Tujia of western Hunan hold a large-scale hand-waving dance every three years. This dance is said to have originated 3,000 years ago, and to have been the prelude to battle.

Traditional folk instruments played for dances.

The Hani

The Hani live in southern Yunnan, dispersed in the Honghe Hani and Yi Autonomous Prefecture, Xishuangbanna Dai Autonomous Prefecture, Jiangcheng Hani and Yi Autonomous County, and the counties of Mojiang and Yuanjiang.

The three dialects of Hani have no written form.

Most of the Hani are engaged in agriculture. Residing in mountainous areas, they are very good at cultivating terraced rice fields on steep slopes.

The Hani are animists, believing that all things on earth have souls. They offer sacrifices to mountains, rivers, dragons and heaven, as well as to their ancestors.

The Hani are mainly engaged in rice cultivation. They are expert builders of terraced paddy fields. Their short skirts and pants are convenient for working in paddy fields.

Hani girls often decorate their hats with silver ornaments.

Young Hani.

Hani girls of Xishuangbanna, Yunnan Province, in their traditional costume.

The Hani also plant tea, contributing to the trade along the ancient "Tea and Horses Route."

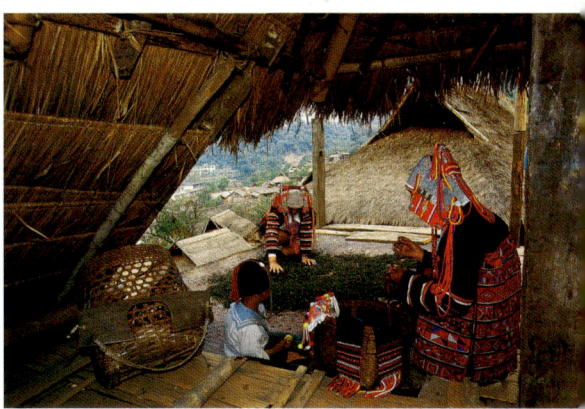

The Kazak

The Kazak are mostly found in Xinjiang Uygur Autonomous Region, with a small number living in Qinghai and Gansu provinces. Traditionally nomadic herders, they are also one of the ten Muslim ethnic groups in China.

The Kazaks are a cheerful people, honest and straightforward in temperament, and extremely hospitable. Their traditional costumes have a distinctive pastoral flavor.

Kazak girls favor brightly colored silk dresses with pleated skirts. A waistcoat is worn over the dress. The cap is decorated with owl feathers.

The Kazaks lead a nomadic life, except in winter, moving between pastures and living in felt tents called yurts.

50

Pasture land in the Tianshan Mountains.

Resting on the way to a new pasture.

Kazak women preparing milk.

Building a yurt.

Kazak women making felt for yurts.

The Li

The Li live in Hainan Province, together with members of the Han, Hui and other ethnic groups. They are a branch of the ancient Baiyue people, and have lived in sub-tropical Hainan Island for over 3,000 years. Many Li speak both the Li and Han languages, the latter of which they use for writing.

The Li are mainly engaged in the cultivation of rice, cotton, tropical fruits and rubber on fertile Hainan Island. Their cotton textile techniques have a long history, and every Li woman is an expert weaver.

The bamboo-skipping dance is a Li tradition. The dancers jump between bamboo sticks which are rapidly separated and clapped together.

Li women are expert weavers, and girls like to wear straight skirts.

傣族 The Dai

The Xishuangbanna Dai Autonomous Prefecture in Yunnan Province has the largest concentration of Dai people. They are mentioned in historical records starting in the first century.

They mainly engage in the cultivation of rice and tropical crops.

The Dai have been followers of the Hinayana sect of Buddhism for over 1,000 years. Every Dai village has its own Buddhist temple, where Buddhist services are held frequently. The Dai have their own spoken and written language. They are unique with their own customs, cuisine, clothing and ornaments.

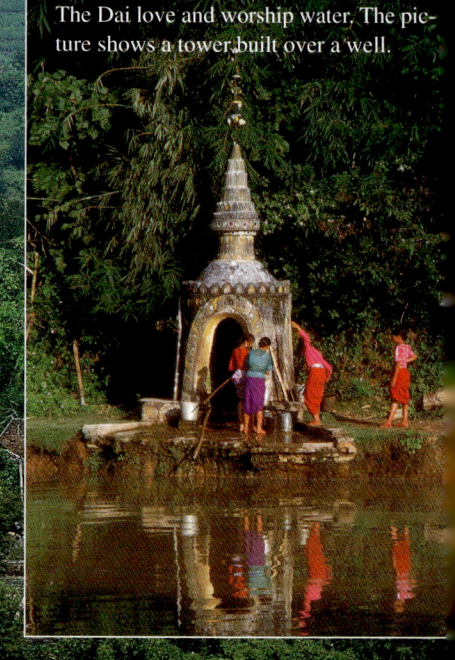

The Dai love and worship water. The picture shows a tower built over a well.

All Dai villages are located in areas of eternal green.

The Water-sprinkling Festival is a joyous occasion for the Dai people.

Traditional costume of the "Flower Waist Dai."

It is said that the Dai bathe 10 times a day.

The Xishuangbanna Dai Autonomous Prefecture in Yunnan Province is home to China's largest Dai community. It has charming tropical rain forest scenery.

傈僳族 The Lisu

Eight centuries ago, the ancestors of the Lisu lived on the upper reaches of the Jinsha River in the northwestern part of Yunnan Province. From the 16th century, they migrated three times, and finally settled in the valleys of the Lancang and Nujiang rivers in Yunnan, mixing with communities of Han, Bai, Nu, Yi and Naxi people. Nowadays, they are mostly concentrated in the Nujiang Lisu Autonomous Prefecture, with some scattered over a dozen or so counties in Yunnan and Sichuan.

The Lisu have their own spoken language, but a script for it was only devised in 1975, based on alphabetical//Latin letters. They are mainly engaged in agriculture, supplemented with food gathering and hunting.

The Lisu are polytheists, believing that all things on earth have souls. Before every important activity, such as reclamation of land, the building of a house or a hunting trip, they invite a sorcerer to perform a divination.

Lisu girls.

The Sword-Pole Festival of the Lisu people falls on the eighth day of the second lunar month.

Participants climb the Sword-Pole in their bare feet.

57

The Va

The Va are mainly located in two Va autonomous counties of Ximeng and Cangyuan in the Ava Mountains of western Yunnan Province.

Most of the Va are engaged in agriculture. They have no written language, and some of them still keep records by cutting notches in sticks and convey messages by showing different objects. A chicken feather, for example, indicates an urgent matter. Banana, sugarcane and salt are offered to visitors from afar to show friendliness.

Traditionally, the Va are animists, but some have been converted to Hinayana Buddhism or Christianity.

The "hair-swaying" dance of the Va girls.

Va girls husking rice, their staple food, using wooden pestles.

Grains are kept in bamboo tubes, which keep moisture, mice and insects away.

Va wooden drum dance.

The She

The She, a minority nationality with a long history, live in scattered communities in the contiguous hilly areas between Guangdong, Fujian, Jiangxi and Zhejiang provinces, in the southeastern part of China. They have mingled with Han people for a long time. They use the Han language.

The She cultivate tea and rice, and also hunt in the forests. The She are excellent singers, and always accompany weddings, funerals, festivals and the reception of guests with songs.

A She girl

The She live in southern Zhejiang Province.

高山族 The Gaoshan

The Gaoshan live on the eastern coast of Taiwan and in mountainous central Taiwan. Only a small number of them live on the mainland of China. According to historical records, the Gaoshan have been living in Taiwan since early in the third century. They have their own spoken language, but no script.

The Gaoshan mainly engage in agriculture, and many of those living by the sea are fishermen. Every year, they hold a ceremony to offer sacrifices to their ancestors. The Gaoshan have retained certain primitive habits and customs.

The popular sport of Spearing the Rattan Ball of the Gaoshan people originated as part of a religious ceremony.

A Gaoshan women.

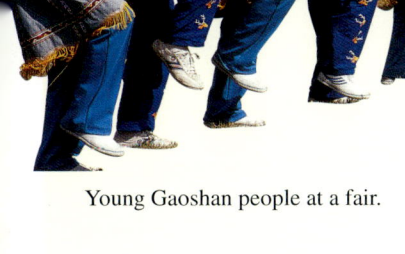

Young Gaoshan people at a fair.

61

拉祜族 The Lahu

Most Lahu live in the Langcang Lahu Autonomous County and Menglian Dai and Lahu Autonomous County in mountainous western Yunnan Province.

The Lahu emerged from the ancient Di and Qiang tribes. From the eighth century to eighteenth century, after a long period of wandering, they finally settled in their present homes, abandoning their nomadic hunting lifestyle to a sedentary farming lifestyle. However, in some areas, the Lahu still engage in slash-and-burn farming, together with food gathering and hunting.

The Lahu have their own language and script, but most of them also speak the Han and Dai languages.

Lahu people celebrating the Kuo Festival.

A young man sends his prospective bride an engagement present.

Lahu women often smoke bamboo water pipes.

A Lahu girl.

The mountainous areas where the Lahu live are rich in bamboo and tea. The pictures show tea pickers and tea being brewed over a charcoal fire.

水族 *The Shui*

The Shui live mainly in Sandu, Libo, Dushan and Duyun in southern Guizhou Province. A small number of them live in the northwestern part of the Guangxi Zhuang Autonomous Region. The Shui are descendents of a branch of the ancient Baiyue tribe.

The Shui homeland is rich in aquatic products, as well as rice, wheat, and cotton. The Shui have their own spoken language. In daily life, they use the Han written language, and their 2,000-year-old script is reserved only for religious occasions.

Looking out of the window.

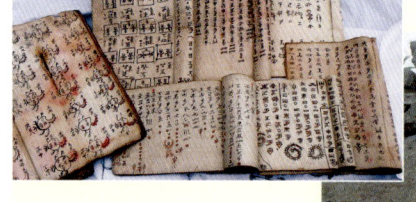

Ancient Shui books.

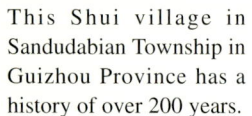

This Shui village in Sandudabian Township in Guizhou Province has a history of over 200 years.

64

The Shui live in finely constructed storied wooden buildings.

Shui girls wear silver ornaments specially for festival days.

"Gaduo" are built on mountain slopes by Shui lovers to pray for a beautiful future.

Shui girls of Dushan, Guizhou Province.

The Dongxiang

The Dongxiang are concentrated at the foot of the mountains south of the Yellow River in the Linxia Hui Autonomous Prefecture, mostly in Dongxiang Autonomous County.

There are two opinions about the origin of the Dongxiang. One opinion holds that they are descendants of Mongolian soldiers stationed at Dongxiang in Hezhou, during the establishment of the Yuan Dynasty in the 13th century. Evidence for this is that their language is close to Mongolian, although they also use the Han language. The other view is that they are descendants of local Hui people who mingled with Mongolian, Han and Tibetan people who arrived in the area later. The Dongxiang are followers of Islam.

The Dongxiang mainly engaged in agriculture, growing potatoes and wheat. The picture shows potato harvesting.

A young Dongxiang couple.

The Naxi

The traditional music of the Naxi preserves the style prevalent during the Tang and Song dynasties.

Ancient hieroglyphic Dongba script.

The Lijiang Naxi Autonomous County and several other counties in Yunnan have the largest concentration of Naxi people, while small numbers of them live in Sichuan and Tibet.

The book *Records of the Historian*, written nearly 2,000 years ago, mentions the Naxi.

The Naxi mainly engage in farming and livestock raising in fertile areas. The Lijiang area boasts advanced trade and handicraft industry. The Naxi have their own spoken language, and use the Han language for writing.

Laihe was once a business hub on the ancient "Tea and Horses Route."

A primitive Naxi dwelling.

The Mosuo people, living in the area of Lugu Lake, are a branch of the Naxi.

The Naxi holy men, called Dongba, are the major transmitters of the Dongba religion and culture.

Residents of the ancient town of Lijiang.

The Jingpo

The Jingpo mainly live in the Dehong Dai and Jingpo Autonomous Prefecture, Yunnan Province. Historical records indicate that the Jingpo originated in the southern part of the Qinghai-Tibet Plateau. They later moved gradually southwards to the northwestern part of Yunnan Province, to the area west of the Nujiang River. In the 16th century, they moved in large numbers to the thickly forested Dehong area, which has a tropical climate.

The Jingpo have their own spoken and written language, but few people use it nowadays. Their culture and costumes remain much the same as when they were formed.

Young Jingpo people in festive mood. Jingpo youngsters favor white turbans, while the old men wear black turbans.

Munao, meaning "everybody dances" in the Jingpo language, is a grand traditional festival of the Jingpo people. It is generally held in the middle of the first lunar month, on an even-numbered day.

Jingpo girls.

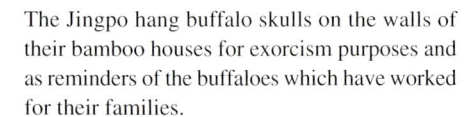

The Jingpo hang buffalo skulls on the walls of their bamboo houses for exorcism purposes and as reminders of the buffaloes which have worked for their families.

The Kirgiz

Most of the Kirgiz live in the Kizilsu Kirgiz Autonomous Prefecture in the southwestern part of Xinjiang Uygur Autonomous Region. The others are scattered in southern and northern Xinjiang and in Fuyu County, Heilongjiang Province.

The ancestors of the Kirgiz lived on the upper reaches of the Yenisey River. In the seventh century, they established close ties with the Tang Dynasty (618-907). Early in the 16th century, they moved in large numbers to the area of the Tianshan and Pamir Mountains. The Kirgiz are Muslims, and are traditionally nomadic herders.

Cutting grass.

Respecting the elderly and loving the young are traditional virtues of the Kirgiz.

Kirgiz women sewing felt for yurts.

A Kirgiz woman in the traditional costume.

The Daur

Most of the Daur live in the Hulun Buir League in Inner Mongolia, and some live in Heilongjiang Province and Xinjiang Uygur Autonomous Region. As they have long mingled with the Mongolian, Ewenki, Oroqen, Han and Kazak peoples, most of the Daur speak more than one language, and their costumes also reflect borrowings from other ethnic groups.

The Daur are descendants of the Kitan, who founded the Liao Dynasty (916-1125). Jiju, a hockey-type game popular in the Liao Dynasty is still played by the Daur.

Most of the Daur farmers, living in Heilongjiang Province, are expert grain growers.

A Daur woman.

土族 The Tu

One third of the Tu live in the Huzhu Tu Autonomous County, in northeast Qinghai Province. The rest are scattered mostly in the eastern part of the province.

Originally nomadic herders, the Tu settled down to farming in the mid-14th century.

The Tu believe in Lamaism. About 60 percent of their native vocabulary is taken from the Mongolian language. As they have no written language of their own, they use Han characters for writing.

Tu girls.

Traditional hospitality.

The colors used in the clothes of Tu women show sharp contrasts. The sleeves in particular are usually pieced together using cloth of five colors.

Tu embroidery.

Displaying hand-made embroideries.

Antiphonal singing between men and women. These songs are called "flower songs."

佬族 The Mulam

The Mulam are descended from the Liao and Ling peoples of the Jin Dynasty (281-420). Most of them live around Luocheng in the Guangxi Zhuang Autonomous Region. The Mulam have their own language, and the majority of them also speak and write the Han language. Some can even speak the language of their Zhuang neighbors. They are followers of Buddhism and Taoism, and believe in the existence of the Heavenly Palace and the Nether World, ghosts and spirits and deified real persons.

Farming is the main occupation of the Mulam. They plant rice, corn, beans and cotton. They mix cinders with white clay to produce earthenware pots, a traditional handicraft.

A Mulam girl going to work in a field.

A bride and bridegroom drink wine from the same cup.

羌族 The Qiang

In historical records, the name Qiang refers to all the nomadic people living in western China in ancient times, and not just a single nationality. As a result of wars and natural calamities, the Qiang people undertook several large-scale migrations from the fourth to the 13th centuries. A branch of them moved into Sichuan Province, and settled in Maowen, Songfan, Wenchuan, Lixian, and other places on the upper reaches of the Minjiang River. Their descendants prospered, and became today's Qiang people.

The areas where the Qiang live are fertile and well watered. As a result, the Qiang are mostly engaged in farming, with a small number also engaged in animal husbandry.

Except for a small number of them who live close to a Tibetan-inhabited area and believe in Lamaism, the Qiang are believers in animism, which holds that all things on earth have a spirit.

A young Qiang woman doing embroidery.

A stone blockhouse in a Qiang village usually has three stories: the upper story for storing grain, the middle story for people to live in, and the lower story for keeping domestic animals.

The ancestors of the Qiang tended sheep. After they migrated into what is now Sichuan Province, they mainly took up farming.

布朗族 *The Blang*

The Blang people live mainly in the Blang, Xiding and Bada mountains in Xishuangbanna, Yunnan Province. There are also scattered Blang communities in Simao and Linchang prefectures in the same province. Anthropological studies show that the Blang, Va and De'ang are all the descendants of the ancient Pu people. Some of the Pu people moved to the plains, and gradually mixed with other nationalities. Those who stayed in the mountains still lived by gathering and hunting, and they formed the principal part of today's Blang.

The Blang live in different areas, and speak two major dialects. They have no written language, and so they use the Dai and Han scripts instead. The Blang are animists, and make sacrificial offerings throughout the year.

The Blang grow cotton and tea, their Pu'er tea being famous both at home and abroad.

A young Blang couple.

An old Blang lady.

The Blang girls wear simple but bright traditional costume and adornments. Their headdresses are often decorated with flowers.

撒拉族 *The Salar*

The ancestors of the Salar migrated from Central Asia to the eastern part of today's Qinghai Province more than 700 years ago. In the course of long historical development, they have merged with the Tibetan, Hui and Han people living around them, and brought into being the Salar nationality, which has its own distinctive culture.

The Salar live mainly in the Xunhua Salar Autonomous County in Qinghai. Irrigated by the Yellow River, this is a fertile land suitable for the growth of crops and fruit trees.

The Salar men are expert wood carvers, who embellish their doors, windows, rafters and colonnades with artistic designs.

An old Salar man entertains guests in his courtyard.

毛南族 The Maonan

The majority of the Maonan people are concentrated in Huanjiang County, in the northern part of the Guangxi Zhuang Autonomous Region, and the rest are scattered in nearby Hechi, Nandan and Yishan counties in Guangxi and Libo County in Guizhou Province. Since the Maonan have for a long time maintained close contacts with the Zhuang and Han people, almost all the Maonan know both the Zhuang and Han languages in addition to their own Maonan language, and write in Han characters.

Most Maonan engage in farming, rice being the major crop. The Maonan people are expert at the handicraft of weaving bamboo articles.

The Wooden-Mask Opera is staged in the fifth lunar month every year during the ceremony for offering sacrifices to the deity Grandpa Sanjie.

Maonan are especially fond of their traditional gaily-decorated bamboo hats. They are also exchanged as love tokens.

锡伯族 *The Xibe*

The Xibe for generations used to live by fishing and hunting on the vast Songhua-Nenjiang Plain and in the Greater and Lesser Xing'an Mountains in northeast China. In 764, the Qing government drafted large numbers of the Xibe and people of some other ethnic minorities from northeast China, and stationed them as guards and cultivators on the northwestern frontier. The ancestors of these people reside in the Xibe Autonomous County of Qapqal and Huocheng and Gongliu counties along the Ili River in the Xinjiang Uygur Autonomous Region. They retain their traditional customs and spoken and written languages, while the Xibe who remain in northeast China, dispersed in different places, are similar to the local Han and Manchu people in language and customs.

Xibe people living in Xinjiang.

The reunion dinner of the Westward Exodus Festival.

86

The Xibe are fond of archery.

The only Xibe-language newspaper published in the Xibe Autonomous County of Qapqal, Xinjiang.

Traditional Xibe patterns for embroidered shoes.

仡佬族 The Gelao

The Gelao people are widely scattered, and there is hardly an all-Gelao village anywhere. They live mainly in Jinshan and Liuzhi counties in western Guizhou Province. A small number of them live in the Longlin Autonomous County in the Guangxi Zhuang Autonomous Region and also in the Wenshan Zhuang and Miao Autonomous Prefecture of Yunnan Province.

Some 2,000 years ago, the Liao people, the ancestors of the Gelao, lived in the Guizhou area, with the men engaged in farming and the women, weaving. In the course of long historical development, the Gelao people gradually became Han in their lifestyle. Today, most of the Gelao use the Han language, and only a few of them can speak the Gelao language. However, they have retained many of their ancient customs and culture.

Young Gelao girls.

On the way to perform the Ground Opera—kind of exorcism. It is called the Ground Opera because it is performed on a piece of flat ground.

The Primi

The Primi live mainly in the Ninglang Yi Autonomous County and Lanping County in northwestern Yunnan Province, with a small number found in Muli and Yanyuan counties in Sichuan Province. The Primi have their own language, but most of them use the Han language.

The ancestors of the Primi were a nomadic tribe on the edge of the Qinghai-Tibet Plateau. Their descendants moved gradually to warmer areas with plenty of water and lush pastures in the southern Xinjiang Uygur Autonomous Region. From the 13th century, they began to settle in the northwestern part of Yunnan Province. The Primi still retain some of the customs and habits of their nomadic ancestors.

Log cabins are the traditional Primi residences.

A Primi woman harvesting.

阿昌族 *The Achang*

The great majority of the Achang live in the western part of Yunnan Province, in the Husa area of Longchuan County and the Zhedao and Dachang areas of Lianghe County.

The ancestors of the Achang lived by gathering and hunting. They began to settle in their present homes and engage in farming in the 13th century. The Achang have their own spoken language. Because they have for a long time lived in mixed communities with Han and Dai people and intermarried with them, most of the Achang also know the Han and Dai languages and use the Han script. Most of the Achang are followers of Hinayana Buddhism.

All Achang women are expert weavers.

Milling flour.

Returning from a local market.

塔吉克族 *The Tajik*

The Tajik nationality has lived for generations in the eastern part of the Pamir Plateau, where the average elevation is 3,000 m. Most of them now live in the Taxkorgan Tajik Autonomous County. In the county's mountain valleys, the Tajik live a semi-nomadic and semi-settled life. They are followers of Islam.

A Tajik girl.

The Tajik people like to play the eagle flute and play the hand drum for the Eagle Dance.

In the upper left picture, people are dressing a bride. The right picture shows a Tajik wedding scene.

The techniques of traditional Tajik handicrafts are passed down from generation to generation.

93

The Nu

The Nu are distributed mainly in Bijiang, Fugong, and Gongshan counties, along the Nujiang River in Yunnan Province.

The Nu have their own language, but no system of writing it. Living in remote areas, the Nu have a backward economy. Even today, some of the Nu still keep records by cutting notches in sticks or by tying knots.

The Nu people worship totems, and each village has its distinctive clan totem. Most of the inhabitants of a Nu village are members of the same clan. The headman of the village is a man of great prestige.

Nu men have a martial bearing.

Plowing an upland field.

Mother and son.

The Nu live in houses made of wooden planks or split bamboo.

乌孜别克族 The Uzbek

In the 13th and 14th centuries, Uzbek traders used to visit Xinjiang from Central Asia. In the 16th century, they began to settle in some cities in Xinjiang. Their numbers increased, until they formed today's Uzbek minority nationality.

As most of the Uzbek are engaged in trade and handicraft industries, the majority of them dwell in Xinjiang's large cities. A small number of Uzbek are engaged in farming and animal husbandry in both southern and northern Xinjiang. The Uzbek are noted for their hospitality.

Young Uzbek women.

188. Weaving a carpet, a traditional Uzbek handicraft.

The Ewenki

The ancestors of the Ewenki used to inhabit the mountain forests northeast of Lake Baikal and the upper reaches of the Heilongjiang River, engaging in fishing, hunting and raising David's deer. In the mid-17th century, they moved to the northeastern part of today's Inner Mongolia Autonomous Region and Nehe County in Heilongjiang Province.

Depending on their geographical environment, some Ewenki are engaged in farming, some in farming-herding and some in animal husbandry. A small number of them still live in the dense forests at the northwestern foot of the Greater Xing'an Mountains, as roving hunters.

The David's deer the Ewenki raise are usually called Sibuxiang. They have the head of a horse, a deer's antlers, a donkey's body and a cow's hooves.

Cooking in the woods.

Animal-skin boots.

The Ewenki are good at using the bark of the birch tree to make a wide variety of household utensils.

David's deer are the main means of transportation for the Ewenki.

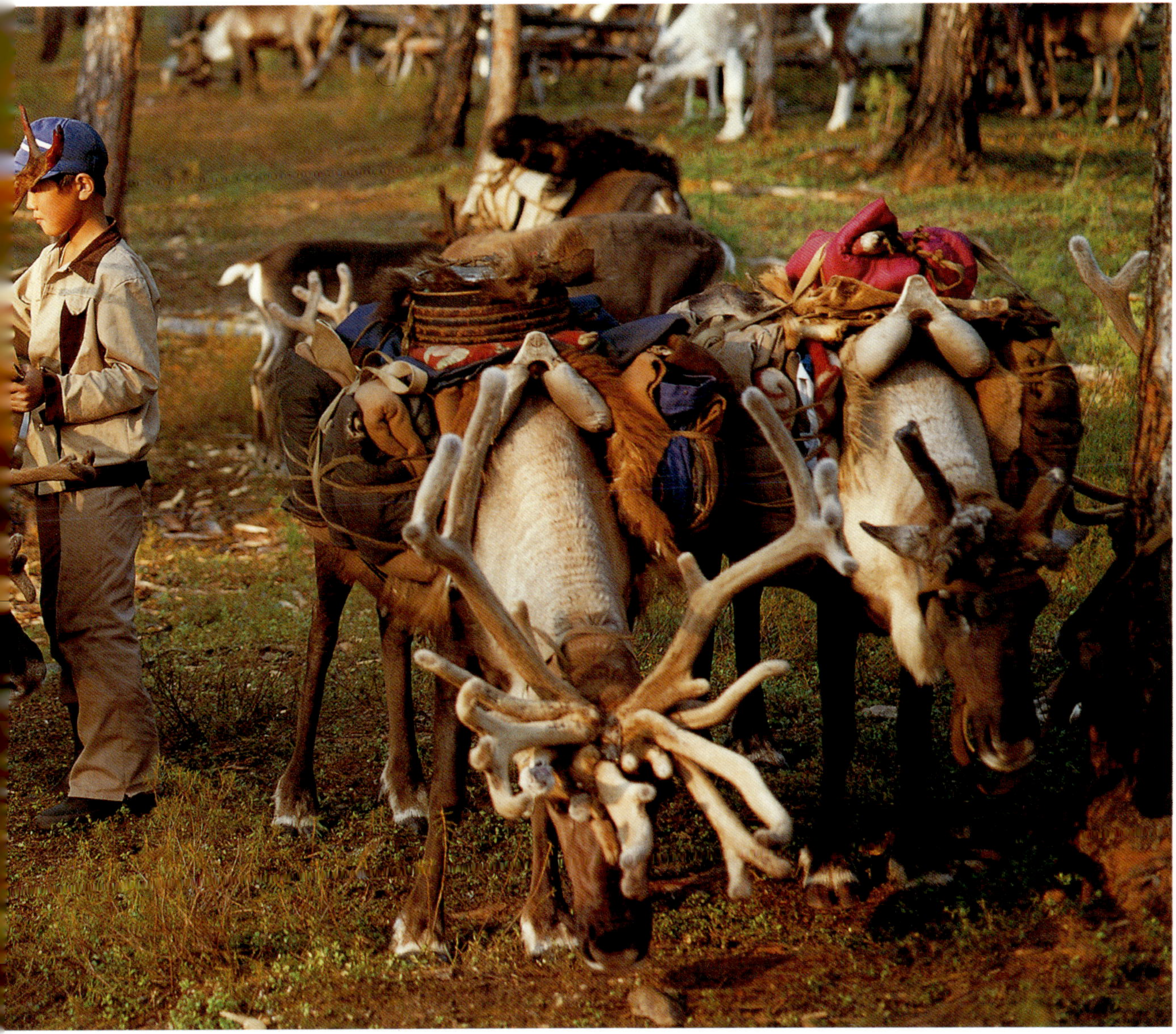

俄罗斯族 The Russians

The ethnic Russians in China are descendants of immigrants from Tsarist Russia from the 18th century on. They live mainly in the cities of Ili, Tacheng, Altay and Urumqi in the Xinjiang Uygur Autonomous Region. There are also a small number of Russians in the Inner Mongolia Autonomous Region and Heilongjiang Province. The Russians form one of the smallest ethnic groups in China.

The ethnic Russians have retained their traditional customs while adopting the ideology, culture and customs of other fraternal ethnic groups in their settlements, especially those of the Han ethnic group.

Little ethnic Russian girls.

An old ethnic Russian farmer living by the Ergun River.

The Bonan

The Bonan live at the northern foot of the Jishi Mountains in western Gansu Province and on the southern bank of the Yellow River. The Bonan, Dongxiang and Salar are close neighbors. They share the same religious beliefs, observe similar customs and live in complete harmony.

After several migrations, the ancestors of the Bonan settled by the Jishi Mountains in the mid-19th century. The climate is gentle in this area and there is plenty of water for irrigation, so it is ideal for both farming and livestock breeding. The Bonan engage in trade and making handicrafts. The Bonan knife is a traditional handicraft article.

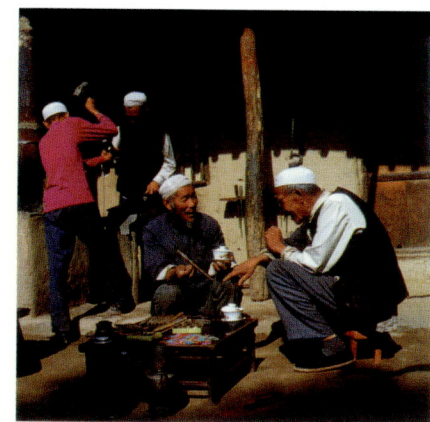

A flowery headpiece worn by Bonan women.

The Bonan knives are famous for their fine craftsmanship both in China and abroad. The Bonan knives are made completely by hand. Here, old Bonan men discuss the finer points of knives.

The De'ang

According to historical records, the De'ang, formerly called the Benglong, are descendants of the Pu people, who lived in Yunnan Province during the Han Dynasty, more than 2,000 years ago. They were called Benglong in the 17th century, and in 1985 they were renamed De'ang.

The De'ang live mainly in the Dehong Dai and Jingpo Autonomous Prefecture and Lincang Prefecture in Yunnan Province. A small number of them are scattered in the areas of Ruili, Lianghe, Longchuan, Baoshan and other places. The sub-tropical region where the De'ang live is ideal for the growth of tea bushes, and the De'ang are famous producers of tea. They have no written language, but have started to use the Han characters.

Weaving cloth.

The De'ang followers of Hinayana Buddhism. There are Buddhist temples and pagodas in almost every village. They also have the tradition of sending boys to serve for a time as monks in the temples. The picture shows a Buddhist ceremony in a De'ang village.

Modern De'ang girls do not shave their hair off any more. They have even dispensed with the turban.

The De'ang women have the tradition of shaving their hair off and covering their heads with turbans decorated with velvet balls. And they also like to wear tubular silver earrings.

裕固族 *The Yugur*

At the northern foot of the Qilian Mountains in central Gansu Province, on the western bank of the Yellow River, lies the Gansu Corridor. This is a 1,000-km-long narrow strip of land, which, from ancient times, was a strategic passage leading from the Central Plains to the West. The Yugur live in the middle of the Gansu Corridor, with 90 percent concentrated in the Yugur Autonomous County of Sun'an.

The Yugur today are mainly herders of livestock, with farming and hunting as sidelines. They are followers of Lamaism. They are historically closely related to the Uygur people of Xinjiang.

The Yugur live in the center of the Gansu Corridor at the foot of the Qilian Mountains.

Yugur women weave ox hair and sheep wool they have produced themselves into felt for making tents known as yurts.

The Yugur costume has been influenced by those of the Tibetans and Mongolians. But their clothes also have their own features. The Yugur women wear waistcoats over their gowns. They wear hats decorated with red tassels and black borders around the brims.

A mobile elementary school on the plain.

A Yugur woman at work.

The Jing

The Jing live mainly on the three small islands known as the Jing islands, off the coast of the Multinational Autonomous County of Fangcheng in the Guangxi Zhuang Autonomous Region. The ancestors of the Jing were immigrants from Vietnam in the early 16th century. Since they have lived for a long time in mixed communities with the Han people, most of the Jing know the spoken and written Han language.

For generations the Jing have lived by fishing. They have also developed a fish-processing industry and the cultivation of pearls and sea horses. The Jing people have a rich knowledge of the sea, and every Jing man is an expert fisherman.

A young Jing man plays the single-string guitar–a traditional Jing musical instrument.

The Jing like to beat drums during the New Year Festival asking for good fortune in the following year.

塔塔尔族 The Tatar

From the early 19th century on, the ancestors of the Tatar trickled into Northwest China from Tsarist Russia, and settled in Xinjiang. They were peasants who had lost their land, tradesmen, intellectuals and religious figures. The Tatar reside mainly in cities of Urumqi, Ining and Tacheng in Xinjiang. Since they have lived for a long time in mixed communities with the Uygur and Kazak, their language is similar to those of these two peoples.

Although people of all ethnic groups are excellent singers and dancers, the Tatar are particularly popular for their songs and dances with distinctive national features.

Music is an indispensable part of the life of the Tatar. Songs often echo in Tatar families.

Tatar children.

独龙族 *The Drung*

In the Drung River Valley in northwestern Yunnan Province live the Drung people. The Drung have their own spoken language, but no written form of it.

The area where the Drung live is covered with dense forests, where many rare birds and animals live. The Drung are mainly hunter-gatherers. Long years of practice have made every Drung man a good hunter. The Drung also fish. Since the Drung River Valley lies in a remote area with poor transportation facilities, the Drung have few contacts with the outside world. As a result, they retain unique and primitive customs and habits.

A Drung girl.

A simple suspension bridge over the Drung River.

109

鄂伦春族 The Oroqen

The Oroqen were one of the last minorities to abandon the life of roving hunters. Before they settled down in the 1950s, the Oroqen lived in the dense virgin forests of the Greater and Lesser Xing'an Mountains extending northward across the eastern part of the Inner Mongolia Autonomous Region and Heilongjiang Province. At that time, their clothing, food, residences, transportation means and customs were dictated by their nomadic life. Their brave and resolute character has been formed by their hard lives in the Greater and Lesser Xing'an Mountains. Today, the Oroqen live mainly in the Oroqen Autonomous Banner of the Hulun Buir League, Inner Mongolia.

Oroqen families now live a settled life.

Houses built by the government for the Oroqen.

Traditional Oroqen handicrafts made of birch bark.

The Oroqen were nomadic hunters in the past.

Historical records show that the Oroqen used to hunt in winter dressed in animal skins.

111

The Hezhen

The Hezhen are the smallest in number of China's 56 nationalities. For generations the Hezhen have lived on the Three-River Plain in Heilongjiang Province, which is bounded by the Songhua, Heilongjiang and Ussuri rivers. This area abounds in marshy land, making it team with wild animals and fish. The Hezhen once were the only nationality in China whose main mode of production was fishing. For a long time, they not only ate fish, but also made clothes, hats and shoes out of fish skin. Hence, they were called the "Fish-skin Tribe."

Aoqi Town, a Hezhen settlement, is located on the bank of the Songhua River.

This photograph of Ge Wenguang's family was taken more than 60 years ago.

112

The Hezhen prize large yellow croakers.

A folk artisan makes fish-skin clothes.

门巴族 The Moinba

The Moinba live in the Moinyu area, and in Megog, Nyingchi and Cona counties, in the southeast of the Tibet Autonomous Region. The area is located in the southern foothills of the Himalaya Mountains, where the climate is warm and humid, dense forests climb halfway up the mountain and fields and trees remain eternally green. Thus it is called "Tibet's Jiangnan [south of the Yangtze River]."

Since the Moinba have long been closely associated with the Tibetans, most of them speak Tibetan, and use the Tibetan script and calendar. Like the Tibetans too, they are believers in Lamaism.

The Moinba entered the era of farming and animal husbandry long ago. Today, they are engaged mainly in farming, with animal husbandry and forestry as sidelines.

A Moinba woman.

Owing to their long tradition of hunting, archery is part of the Moinba way of life.

洛巴族 The Lhoba

The Lhoba women are pipe smokers.

The Lhoba people live in the Zayu, Menyu and Milin areas at the foot of the Himalaya Mountains in southeastern Tibet.

Until the 1950s, the Lhoba remained at the primitive stage of slash-and-burn farming, gathering and hunting. In the last few decades, economic conditions have greatly improved for the Lhoba.

The Lhoba are animists, believing that all things on earth have a spirit. Consequently, on the occasion of a wedding, funeral, sowing or traveling, the Lhoba will kill a hen to divine what the outcome will be.

基诺族 *The Jino*

The Jino people live in the Jinoluoke Mountains in Jinghong County, Yunnan Province, an area known for its mild climate and plentiful rainfall. The Jino have a spoken language, but no written language.

The Jino area abounds in rice, cotton, tea, bananas, papayas and many kinds of medicinal herbs. The Jino engage mainly in farming, with gathering and hunting as sidelines. They worship gods and spirits, and sacrificial ceremonies are many and frequent. Before taking any important action, the Jino will practice divination.

Typical Jino waist-loom for cloth weaving.

A young Jino woman.

The Qiek, a traditional Jino musical instrument, is made of bamboo.

At a wedding ceremony, an older relative locks the bride and bridegroom together with a "lovers' lock."

The big drum dance. The big drum is regarded as a divine instrument by the Jino. According to legend, when the Jino area was inundated by a flood, the ancestors of the Jino survived by holding on to a big drum.

The people of a Jino village celebrate the Temaoke Festival.

Administrative Map of China

图书在版编目（CIP）数据

中国少数民族/兰佩瑾编.－北京：外文出版社，2003.3
（中华风物）
ISBN 7-119-03184-8

Ⅰ.中… Ⅱ.中… Ⅲ.少数民族－概况－中国－英文 Ⅳ.D633.3

中国版本图书馆CIP数据核字(2002)第077933号

《中华风物》编辑委员会

顾　　问：	蔡名照	赵常谦	黄友义	刘质彬
主　　编：	肖晓明			
编　　委：	肖晓明	李振国	田　辉	房永明
	呼宝珉	胡开敏	崔黎丽	兰佩瑾
前　　言：	邢　莉			
内　　文：	廖　频	余冰清	兰佩瑾	
摄　　影：	杜殿文	谢　军	刘思功	李春生
	成为东	李植森	兰佩瑾	丹　增
	刘建明	申　军	高明义	蒋　剑
	袁学军	孙永学	等	
翻　　译：	王　琴	欧阳伟萍		
英文定稿：	郁　苓			
设　　计：	元　青	等		
责任编辑：	兰佩瑾			

中国少数民族

© 外文出版社
外文出版社出版
（中国北京百万庄大街24号）
邮政编码：100037
外文出版社网页：http://www.flp.com.cn
外文出版社电子邮件地址：info@flp.com.cn
sales@flp.com.cn
天时包装（深圳）有限公司印刷
中国国际图书贸易总公司发行
（中国北京车公庄西路55号）
北京邮政信箱第399号　邮政编码 100044
2003年(24开)第一版
2003年第一版第一次印刷
（英文）
ISBN 7-119-03184-8/J·1624（外）
05800（精）
85-E-554S